SCREEN SANITY

WRITTEN BY **Krista Boan + Tracy Foster**
Co-Founders of START

DESIGNED BY **Kristen Sobba**

To order additional copies of this resource visit **westartnow.org/resources** or email at **info@westartnow.org.**

Second Edition 2021 | Copyright © 2021 We Start Now

TABLE OF CONTENTS

WHAT'S INSIDE

MAIN COURSE

OPTIONAL / DIVE DEEPER

WELCOME

Today's parents have many resources to help them prepare to raise a child, but there's one book that doesn't yet exist: *What To Expect When You're (Tech)xpecting!* The truth is, we are all pondering questions like "How much screen time is too much? When do I get my child a phone? How should I prepare them for social media?"

We get it--a few years back, we began asking the same questions for our own children, and gathering fresh ideas to help families tackle some of the most common screentime challenges. We've bundled our favorites here for you—but we know tips and tricks are not enough. Because in thousands of conversations with parents, one theme has risen to the top:

Raising kids in this digital world is hard, but it's even harder to do it alone.

What parents need, more than ever, are other parents to link arms with. Our greatest desire for this study is that you'll have rich, honest conversations with others who will cheer you on as you pursue digital health.

The beautiful thing? This is going to look all kinds of ways. Some of you around a kitchen table with your book club, some with your PTA in the school library...you can even do it by yourself after the kids are tucked into bed. Some parents of teens, some parents of toddlers. Grandparents. Coaches. Teachers. Caregivers. Co-workers.

Whoever you are—wherever you meet—we are grateful to be on this journey beside you. Together, let's build a world where kids stay captivated by life, not screens.

Yours,
Krista Boan + Tracy Foster | START Co-Founders

HOW TO ACCESS THE VIDEOS

Use your smartphone's camera app to scan here.

A link will pop up that takes you to our members only page.
Enter your email to access the video library.

If you run into technical snags, please reach out and let us know!
Email **info@westartnow.org** and we'll get you back up and running

In this guide, you'll find ten videos designed to spark rich conversations for groups of people. **You'll want to unpack the content with three simple steps:**

1 WATCH THE VIDEO

Each session's corresponding video should be viewed before moving on to the discussion. To watch the video, scan the QR code on page 6—or visit **westartnow.org/screen-sanity-portal.** Enter your email, and you'll be given access to the video library on our members only website. At the end of each video, take time to pause, reflect, and jot down a note or two before you turn the page.

2 DISCUSS THE QUESTIONS

After the video, dig in to the discussion questions together. We are all fighting battles with screentime—so we invite you to **make your group a no-judgment zone.** Stay curious, honest, and kind as you engage with the content and listen to stories from others in your group.

3 EXPLORE THE ADDITIONAL RESOURCES

The questions that will surface are tough, and you might not know all the answers. You might even end up with more questions! We've included some of our favorite resources and perspectives to help you continue to unpack the topic at hand.

You'll find tips for every age and stage sprinkled throughout the content. If a video speaks to a stage of life you aren't currently in, we invite you to just listen and learn. **Don't feel like you need to do everything discussed**—just do what makes sense for your family. Focus less on broad, sweeping changes and more on small, do-able takeaways.

VIDEO 01 /
THEN&NOW

We are the first generation of parents raising digital natives. There is no handbook for the challenges we are facing.

We are the wisdom makers.

Use your smartphone's camera app to

SCAN HERE TO WATCH **VIDEO 01**

or go to westartnow.org/screen-sanity-portal

SESSION**RECAP**

The core challenges our kids face today are not much different from the ones in the world we grew up in. **Disappointment. Grief. Loneliness.** And yet, the way we experience these challenges is very different.

PAUSE**+REFLECT**

What stood out to you?

GROUP**DISCUSSION 01**

How are our children's lives today better than you imagined they would be?

How are they more challenging?

GROUP**DISCUSSION 02**

The side effects we are seeing with screens are accidental — no parent has ever handed their child a phone hoping they would get bumped, bruised, or even destroyed by it.

What's one side-effect that concerns you most — either for yourself or with your kids?

TAKE HOME TIP
TELL FAMILY STORIES

More than 90% of teenagers and young adults can retell family stories when asked, even if they seemed uninterested when stories were told.

Next time you share stories about your childhood, try including the hard, gritty moments alongside the highlights. In doing so, you model the emotional awareness, perseverance and resilience you want them to develop as they live out their own stories.

2018 Emory Study

It's harder to be a parent than ever before because it's harder to be a teenager than ever before.

From the relentless pressures of social comparison to darker hazards like cyberbullying, sexting, violent pornography and online predators, it's easy to understand how the rates of depression, anxiety and suicide have been steadily increasing for the next generation.

And to exacerbate these challenges, a recent DoSomething.org survey revealed that

Only 14% of youth say they have had a good conversation with an adult about the online world.

Whether you feel like it or not, you have what it takes to be a mentor and guide to your child—even in the digital world. This won't be through the tap of an easy button, or a list of apps to avoid...or a magical number of screentime minutes...because those recommendations will change overnight.

We won't ask you to do a total overhaul of your family's screentime—but in the sessions ahead, we'll offer you a set of digital health principles that will hopefully bring a little screen sanity into your family life.

"Phones and apps aren't good or bad by themselves...

but for adolescents who don't yet have the emotional tools to navigate life's complications and confusions, they can exacerbate the difficulties of growing up: learning how to be kind, coping with feelings of exclusion, taking advantage of freedom while exercising self-control. It's more important than ever to teach empathy from the very beginning, because our kids are going to need it."

MELINDA GATES

VIDEO 02 /
START WITH YOURSELF

We recently asked teens what the number one thing is that adults could do for kids' mental health. Their answer?

Put your phones down and talk to us.

Use your smartphone's camera app to
SCAN HERE TO WATCH VIDEO 02

or go to westartnow.org/screen-sanity-portal

SESSION**RECAP**

Technology companies use powerful techniques to keep us glued to our phones and this can accidentally interfere with the things that matter most to us. It's worthwhile to pause and consider what matters most in our lives and use friction to help us reduce unhealthy habits so we can **model digital health for our kids.**

PAUSE**+REFLECT**

What stood out to you?

GROUP**DISCUSSION 01**

Before you discuss, take a look at the list of values to the right and pick 3-5 that are important to you. Then, share an example of technology maximizing your values and an example of technology interfering with your values.

For example: *Sometimes Facebook supports my core value of connection, while other times it interferes with my core value of productivity.*

GROUP**DISCUSSION 02**

When it comes to creating a healthy screen-life balance, it is helpful to identify the tricks tech companies use to keep us glued to our phones.

What is one tip you've tried that helps you resist these tactics, keeping your tech in check?

TAKE HOME TIP
YOU GO FIRST

Casually survey your kids about what they think matters most to your family.

And then, if you are feeling brave, ask your kids what they notice about your device use—and whether it sometimes gets in the way of living out what matters most to your family. Don't defend yourself; just listen with curiosity. Take note of ways technology is interfering with the things that you value most, and experiment with small tweaks in your digital habits.

You don't have to strive for perfection, but stepping into the arena first will give you major street cred as you talk with your kids about screentime struggles—and empathy for the world they are navigating.

If you don't stand for something, you'll fall for anything.

What 3-5 values matter most to your family?

- ☐ Achievement
- ☐ Balance
- ☐ Commitment
- ☐ Community
- ☐ Connection
- ☐ Creativity
- ☐ Discipline
- ☐ Empathy
- ☐ Encouragement
- ☐ Exploration
- ☐ Faith
- ☐ Friendship
- ☐ Giving
- ☐ Grace
- ☐ Gratitude

- ☐ Hard Work
- ☐ Honesty
- ☐ Honor
- ☐ Kindness
- ☐ Love
- ☐ Productivity
- ☐ Recreation
- ☐ Respect
- ☐ Self-Improvement
- ☐ Service
- ☐ Sustainability
- ☐ Teamwork
- ☐ Tolerance
- ☐ Trust
- ☐ _____

ADDITIONAL**RESOURCES**

BREAKING UNHEALTHY PHONE HABITS

1   **Turn off notifications that aren't from real people.**

Those tempting little dings that invite us to just take "one quick peek"—unless they're from a real person (like texts or calls).

2   **Filter the noise with a watch.**

For some of us, the number one reason we carry our phone in our pocket is because we need to be "on call" for the people who depend on us. One helpful trick is to use a smartwatch as a tool to filter out notifications from everyone except the few people who need to get through to you — like spouses, caregivers, and the school nurse.

3   **Give your phone a spring cleaning.**

For many of us, clutter isn't just found in the closets of our homes—it also gathers in the corners of our phones. That person we follow on Instagram who makes us feel bad about our own lives? It's okay to unfollow them. That app that steals our time and attention? Try deleting it (or moving it off your home page). Give yourself permission to get rid of things that don't spark joy.

4   **Apply friction.**

One of the best ways to adopt healthy habits is to insert different types of friction into your daily routine. Consider what tiny obstacles you can put in place to make it a little harder to mindlessly reach for your screen. Whether it is keeping your phone in your desk drawer to increase your concentration at work or leaving it in your car when you go out to eat, get creative about ways you can disrupt bad screen habits and adopt healthier ones.

OUR SOCIAL DILEMMA

Netflix Documentary // The Social Dilemma

What are the consequences of our growing dependence on social media? As digital platforms become a lifeline to stay connected, Silicon Valley insiders reveal how social media is reprogramming civilization by exposing what's hiding on the other side of your screen.

Available on Netflix

Screen Sanity Podcast // Episode 9

Max Stossel joins us from the Center for Humane Technology and together, we unpack the "secret sauce" tech companies build into our devices to keep us hooked...and dream about a world where kids measure success—not in views, likes or comments—but by the value they add to people's lives

Listen along at **westartnow.org/podcast**

Looking to prepare your kids to navigate our social dilemma? Here are four big words to teach them!

Attention Economy—The more time you spend on your screen, the more money advertisers make. Tech companies build powerful brain tricks into their apps, most of which are VERY effective, even if they take you down a different path than you intended to go.

Variable Rewards—When you check your social media and gaming feeds, you SOMETIMES get a reward. Not every time, just sometimes. This unpredictability makes it tempting to keep checking in.

Algorithms—Really, really smart chefs behind the screen using a really, really tasty recipe, in order to serve you the perfect next thing on your screen that you can't resist watching.

Social Media Echo Chambers—When an algorithm learns what content has grabbed your attention, it will push you towards more extreme versions of whatever you view. You end up in a digital village with people who are the same as you, and you have fewer opportunities to learn about the other side of the story. To curb this, try following people in your feeds who are different than you. Better yet? Initiate curious, open-minded conversations with different people who can help you see the world from their shoes.

VIDEO 03 /
TABLES&BEDTIMES

Just like our devices, we need to ~~recharge.~~

There are many places you can establish as "device-free zones" but if you are looking for a place to start, we recommend meal tables and bedtimes.

Use your smartphone's camera app to
SCAN HERE TO WATCH VIDEO 03

or go to westartnow.org/screen-sanity-portal

SESSION**RECAP**

Habits of unplugging and recharging can promote mental health throughout your children's lives, and one of the best ways to develop these habits is to have consistent, predictable device-free zones as a family. There are lots of ways to do this, but if you are looking for a couple of places to start **we suggest tables and bedtimes.**

PAUSE**+REFLECT**

What stood out to you?

GROUP**DISCUSSION 01**

Are there times and spaces where you hope to create device-free zones?

☐ Bedrooms

☐ Bathrooms

☐ During meals

☐ Meetings at work

☐ Vacations

☐ Family outings

☐ In the car (except long trips)

☐ Sports practice

☐ Before school/work

☐ During school

☐ Pool/playground

☐ _____

If you are choosing bedrooms, when will devices go to sleep? Where will they charge?

Bedtime

☐ ____ minutes before bed

☐ 1 hour before bed

☐ 8:00 p.m.

☐ 9:00 p.m.

Where

☐ Kitchen

☐ Parent's room

☐ Home office

☐ _____

GROUP**DISCUSSION 02**

When we establish device-free zones, we are developing lifelong habits that will foster our kids' mental health. And when the whole community is on board, it is a game-changer.

When parent communities adopt a digital curfew— where devices are plugged in to recharge outside of kids' bedrooms—FOMO goes down, sleep goes up and risky behaviors aren't as tempting. When coaches challenge players to keep phones stowed in gear bags during games or practice, athletes are better able to keep their eyes on the ball. Though they'll likely protest mightily at first, kids are often relieved to be released from the pressure to always be "on."

What are creative, non-judgmental ways we can inspire others to opt-in? Is there a space or event where you are thinking about leading the charge?

TAKE HOME TIP
DEVICE-FREE GATHERINGS

The next time you host a playdate, sleepover, or mixer, consider making it device-free.

Our #1 tip? Make it clear in the advertising or invitations that there will be a device check-in station.

Maybe try this language: "We're looking forward to our get together! Just a quick note to let you know phones will be in a basket, collected at the beginning of the party. If the kids need to reach you, they can come to the station and use their phone." This heads up prevents guest from being caught off guard when they arrive to the event.

ADDITIONAL**RESOURCES**

OUR DAUGHTER'S NIGHTLY STRUGGLE *by* Allison | START Parent

My daughter is 16 and, like all teens, deals with social drama and ups and downs. I wanted her to have a phone for safety, but last year I began to realize that she was using it for much more than that. She was staying up late at night texting and on social media, and the beautiful daughter I knew and loved was, quite frankly, becoming awful to live with.

After investigating her hours of late night phone use (which for a technology challenged mom like myself was no easy task), my husband and I decided it was time for us to start putting her device in our room at bedtime. I honestly had no idea how much this decision would impact her. After she blew up in anger, she began sobbing and puddled on the floor. As I held her, I just listened. Listened to all the worries and fears of fitting in and keeping up, but there was something even more alarming keeping her up at night...my daughter had been counseling another teen late at night who was suicidal. Her huge heart had been on high alert. She HAD to stay up and be available at all times "in case" her friend needed her.

We were able to talk, really talk, (well, she talked and I held my breath hoping that it wouldn't stop). She shared all her social circle drama, the comments on social media she had to keep up with, the sleep overs and parties she saw that she knew she wasn't invited to, and most importantly how she was single handedly owning responsibility for her friend's life. My teen was relieved when we talked through how to break the silence and get her friend help, real help, and that it wasn't my daughter's responsibility to carry that burden, especially not alone. Together we came up with a plan to involve adults who can support her friend and break the silence over suicidal thoughts.

After the dust settled and we stuck to our new "no phone at bedtime" rule, I was amazed at the changes we saw. I could tell that my girl was so relieved! Much like setting limits with a curfew, she needed that structure from us to take the pressure off. Also, while initially it was an adjustment for all of us at bedtime to take the phone (not going to lie, some days were harder than others depending on what was going on socially), after a while it became routine. She began to use our limits to protect herself too, telling peers her mom and dad were taking the phone (we gave her permission to blame us for any lame-ness). She got sleep, she was less irritable and I saw my beautiful girl come back.

Navigating this technology thing is not fun, for parents or our teens. But I will fight for our daughter's health, and am happy to report that this **battle was worth it.**

Visit **WESTARTNOW.ORG/BLOG** for more ideas on how to improve your family's digital health.

DEVICE-FREE ZONES OUTSIDE THE HOME

A Case for Restricting Phones in Schools

As a high school principal, Scott Bacon has a sobering understanding of the impact of screentime on the lives of his students. In Episode 4 of the Screen Sanity Podcast, you'll hear real-life wisdom from someone who spends every day on the front lines.

Listen along at **westartnow.org/podcast**

Phone Boundaries in After-School Programs

Angie Daniels is the Program Manager for The Hope Center where she works to provide a family-like atmosphere for kids. In Episode 8 of the Screen Sanity Podcast, Angie shares how boundaries with technology have led to a flourishing, vibrant culture.

Listen along at **westartnow.org/podcast**

Teams + Screens: Keeping Their Eyes on the Ball

When we think of youth sports, we think of water coolers, bleacher buns, sunflower seeds, sunburns and trophies. But in recent years, a new player on the field: the smartphone. This blog post is a great read to share with families on your team.

Check it out at **westartnow.org/blog**

Device Free Board Rooms

This blog post shares examples from companies who are taking device-free zones to heart and experimenting with new workplace practices to support digital wellness, including Netsmart—a healthcare company based in Kansas City.

Check it out at **westartnow.org/blog**

VIDEO 04 /
ACCOUNTABILITY

There are no internet filtering solutions that are 100% foolproof

but you'll feel better with these measures in place. **Think of them like a seatbelt** — offering you as much protection as possible from accidents in the online world.

Use your smartphone's camera app to

SCAN HERE TO WATCH VIDEO 04

or go to westartnow.org/screen-sanity-portal

SESSION**RECAP**

While the hazardous topics of pornography and online predators are not for the faint of heart, they are critical discussions for parents who want to **keep their kids safe in the online world.** We can help our kids navigate this by using gated streaming sources when possible, avoiding using devices in private, installing filters as safety nets, and having open, honest conversations. If we do not guide them, make no mistake, the internet will.

PAUSE**+REFLECT**

What stood out to you?

GROUP**DISCUSSION 01**

If you've tried an internet filtering product, or if you've had the "porn talk" with your child, share about the experience with the group.

What worked? What was challenging?
What recommendations do you have?

GROUP**DISCUSSION 02**

One of the greatest challenges facing parents today is starting a conversation with another adult about internet access/filters in their home during playdates, sleepovers, etc.

If you've started this conversation, share what you learned.

TAKE HOME TIP
BE PREPARED

Do you remember the Just Say No Campaign from the 80s and 90s? It encouraged a simple response to peer pressure: Just say "no." Despite billions of dollars spent, it did not work.

In the same way, today's kids will almost certainly be pressured for nudes, so rather than "just saying no," **it's important to help your child brainstorm how they will respond to nude requests.**

One girl shared she responds by texting a nude image of a Barbie doll. Another girl shared she texts a black square with the caption "Here I am nude, in the dark." Maybe your teen just wants to shoot straight, saying, "I'm not in for that." Or maybe something sassy, "Um...no, a picture can't do it justice."

Few thoughts are as daunting to parents as the prevalence of pornography and predators in the lives of modern kids. While we'd like to think it mostly lives in hard-to-reach corners of the internet, the reality is that it's only a few clicks away.

In fact, the average age of first pornography exposure is 9.* While it does take a little time and attention to install these safety layers,

you'll sleep much better knowing they are in place.

1 Base Layer

Internet filters at the router level, to keep hardcore content out of your child's Google searches: Cleanbrowsing DNS, Open DNS, Gryphon, Circle.

2 Second Layer

Filtering and monitoring at the device level, for times when devices leave your wifi: Covenant Eyes, Canopy and Bark, which scan social media and text feeds, alerting you when there is harmful content.

3 Third Layer

Know mistakes will happen. When your child shares a shocking situation, it's best if you've practiced your "I'm not shocked face." Use language like "Tell me more. I'm listening."

* Defend Young Minds

ADDITIONAL**RESOURCES**

WEAR YOUR SEATBELT

The online world can be exciting to explore — but on this digital highway, hazards abound. Predators, bullies and porn bots are sure to cross your child's path, and there are few safety measures built in to protect them from harm. **Here are some precautions your kids can take when they open a new social media or gaming account.**

Safety nets to put in place:

☐ Setting accounts to private   ☐ Blocking messages from strangers

☐ Turning off location   ☐ _____

When inappropriate content comes across the screen, I'll teach my child to:

☐ Look away   ☐ Let parents know (we promise to not overreact)

☐ Toggle to homescreen   ☐ _____

When a password gets created/updated, I want my child to let me know via:

☐ Text   ☐ Email   ☐ Post-it   ☐ Updating family password list

When someone asks for a nude text, here's a creative way they can "say no":

_____

_____

_____

UNCOMFORTABLE CONVERSATIONS

In Episode 7 of the Screen Sanity Podcast, Rob and Zareen Cope share how they've navigated uncomfortable conversations about sleepovers, playdates...and porn. Listen in to learn more about the harm that porn is causing a generation and practical ideas for protecting and educating our kids.

Listen along at **westartnow.org/podcast**

It's hard to keep track of everything our kids are into, let alone know how to talk about them. Our Parent Guides are here to help. These downloadable PDFs will give you the skinny on today's hottest apps and trends including TikTok, Snapchat, cyberbullying, porn and other topics to help you train them to drive cautiously in the digital world. Great for sharing with caregivers.

Grab your downloads at **westartnow.org/parent-guides**

Filmmakers Rob and Zareen Cope share their journey in "Our Kids Online" a documentary that zooms in on the topics of pornography and predators in a safe and enlightening way. The visuals in this film are NOT graphic, but the stories and stats shared are definitely PG-13, so plan to watch without your kids.

Available to rent at **ourkidsonline.info.**

Good Pictures Bad Pictures is a read-aloud story about a mom and dad who explain what pornography is, why it's dangerous, and how to reject it. This internationally-acclaimed book engages young kids to porn-proof their own brains. There is also junior version from children ages 3-6.

Available on Amazon.

VIDEO 05 /
RIDE. PRACTICE. DRIVE.

When you teach your kids to drive, you

don't simply hand them the keys and wish them luck.

You prepare them to navigate risky situations and road hazards through driver's ed. Take this same approach in the digital world.

Use your smartphone's camera app to

SCAN HERE TO WATCH **VIDEO 05**

or go to westartnow.org/screen-sanity-portal

SESSION**RECAP**

Device introduction should ideally be an intentional process that starts with limited freedom and grows slowly as they demonstrate competence. **With devices and apps, start simple, with limited options.** When it's time for something new, coach them from the passenger seat. Once they master one skill, give them something more complex to try. Eventually, kids learn to be self-regulated, independent drivers.

PAUSE**+REFLECT**

What stood out to you?

GROUP**DISCUSSION 01**

Share about your experiences with introducing new apps or devices—or being surprised when they "introduced themselves." **What worked? What was challenging? Would you recommend these products?**

GROUP**DISCUSSION 02**

In the session, we learned that our goal is self-regulated, independent smartphone drivers. **If we were to fast forward our childrens' lives 10-15 years, what do you most hope they will have learned about using a smartphone?**

TAKE HOME TIP
WEIGHING SAFETY + INDEPENDENCE

With the help of technology, today's children are kept safer, make fewer mistakes, and are shielded from unpleasant outcomes. From location trackers to online grade portals, we can instantly know where our kids are, see what they're doing, know how they're performing and jump on any perceived failures.

But it's worth noting that sometimes this backfires, as kids don't develop the coping mechanisms necessary to handle stress and pressure as adults.

While we don't recommend throwing your child into the deep end without swimming lessons, **we challenge you to sprinkle in opportunities for autonomy as your child spreads their wings, especially in low risk situations.** It can be uncomfortable to take an occasional break from tracking, but it might be the taste of independence and self-regulation they need to flourish in adulthood.

SMARTPHONE ROADMAP

When buying a device, first consider what level of functionality your kid actually needs—then buy a device that meets the needs but avoids exposure to mature experiences.

1 ### Phase One

Walkie Talkie Allows kids to experiment with independence, while giving parents peace of mind because there is no screen to worry about. A brilliant way to develop conversation skills and boost social-emotional development.

2 ### Phase Two

Gizmo or Gabb Watches Good for kids who are ready for some independence, but not ready for the responsibility of a phone. GPS tracking, step-counting and parent-approved limited calling and texting allow parents to call or text to check in.

3 ### Phase Three

Gabb Z2 or Pinwheel First Phone For kids who are ready for the basic features of a phone, but not wanting the stigma of a flip phone. Gabb's basic plan comes with limited features like calls, texts (no photos), camera, calendar and calculator. For a phone with a larger menu of kid-friendly apps, check out the Pinwheel.

4 ### Phase Four

Strip down a smartphone When it's time to move to a smartphone, remember it will be much easier to start with strong limits and release them slowly. Invest time stripping it of unnecessary or risky features/apps, and use our Smartphone Toolkit to help guide a conversation about smartphone expectations.

ADDITIONAL**RESOURCES**

HANDING OVER THE KEYS?

When it's time for a smartphone learner's permit, it's important to set clear expectations from the get-go. Not sure where to start? **We've got you covered!** Our Smartphone Toolkit is designed to help you get started on the right foot as you navigate this new territory. Download your copies at westartnow.org/smartphone-toolkit.

Smartphone Rules of Thumb

When it comes to setting boundaries with new devices, it is much easier to start with strong limits and release them slowly rather than trying to put them in place during a time of stress. In this downloadable PDF, we've put together five topics to talk about when it's time for a phone.

Download your copy at **westartnow.org/resources**

Smartphone Plan

A worksheet for parents and kids to fill out together, this plan helps to guide your conversation about smartphone expectations. Perfect to pair with our Smartphone Rules of Thumb!

Download your copy at **westartnow.org/resources**

Smartphone Tech Topics

Use these cards to strike up a conversation with your tween or teen about smartphone expectations. Have fun, stay curious and try to see the world through each other's eyes. Your goal? Deepened trust and empathy – a firm foundation for the road ahead.

Download your copy at **westartnow.org/resources**

COACHING FROM THE PASSENGER SEAT

It's easy to believe that because our kids seem so tech-savvy and are on screens so much, they will leave our homes with marketable tech skills. However, employers are finding that often isn't true. We loved these tips from Melissa Griffin, also known as "HR Mom," who has developed internship programs at companies like Petco and Nationwide.

1   **Have them conduct basic internet research for you**
Have them research the best way to kill weeds or find the cheapest price for fence replacement. Have them find the cheapest rental car and hotel for your vacation. Talk to them about how reservations and insurance work and have them call to reserve it. Let them fumble and make mistakes on the call while you're there to coach and encourage them.

2   **Have them call to schedule their own haircuts, doctor and dentist appointments, and dog grooming**
Again, if they sound dumb or forget to say or ask something, no problem! If they learned something, it was a success!

3   **Have them complete your online curbside pickup grocery order**
They can look in the pantry and add items your family needs and you can revise when they're done. Maybe they can own this and have it completed every Friday night (for example). Give them a weekly budget. This will teach them how much groceries actually cost. Meeting deadlines and budget limitations are real-life job skills.

4   **Teach them how to use Microsoft Excel**
They can use it to make a packing list for your next vacation. Ask them to color code items for each person and have them pack their own bags. Have them track income of their lawn-mowing job or summer camp fundraising. When the use of technology is practical, they'll learn it twice as fast and it will stick!

5   **Have them make PowerPoint presentations for Grandma's birthday or Father's Day, etc.**
You'll be surprised how much time they'll put into these and how quickly they learn how to use animation and graphics. One of my favorite Mother's Day memories includes watching a funny slideshow created for me by my 8-year-old.

47

Visit **HRMOM.COM** for more ideas on leading and launching real-world ready kids.

VIDEO 06 /
TIME WELL SPENT

The digital world wants you to keep scrolling but at the end of your life, all you have is your time and attention.

What will you say was time well spent?

Use your smartphone's camera app to
SCAN HERE TO WATCH **VIDEO 06**

or go to westartnow.org/screen-sanity-portal

SESSION**RECAP**

Time well spent often includes activities in the offline world that foster personal growth—including games, chores, outdoor time and even boredom! But it also includes finding meaningful ways to connect in the online world— taking interest in their favorite apps, using Zoom or Facetime to have real-time interaction, and **choosing screentime that helps you create and connect rather than consume.**

PAUSE**+REFLECT**

What stood out to you?

GROUP**DISCUSSION 01**

As you reflect on your own childhood, what moments stick out to you as Time Well Spent?

Share with the group why they were meaningful.

GROUP**DISCUSSION 02**

The pandemic was a forced opportunity to pause and rethink everything—including how we define time well spent in a post-pandemic world. Maybe this meant a new activity or routine you put into practice as a family or a calendar commitment you shed as your realize it wasn't worth your time.

Maybe it's a lesson you personally learned through the challenges of social distancing...or a way you saw your kids growing through this time of adversity. **Share one of your pandemic takeaways.**

GROUP**DISCUSSION 03**

Raising kids to pursue digital health is hard, but it's even harder to do it alone.

Is there a group of people who you want to share Screen Sanity with? What do you need to make that happen?

(Psst...check out pages 92-97 for tips to help you get started!)

In our rush to keep up with the Kardashians, we've forgotten how to keep up with each other.

TAKE HOME TIP
BRING SCREENTIME TO LIFE

While it can be tempting to remove all screentime from your definition of "time well spent," one of the most forward-thinking things you can do as a parent is to step into your child's digital world, seeing it through their eyes. Ask your child to give you a tour of his or her Minecraft world. Surprise your tween by learning a TikTok dance. If your kids love the epic YouTubers Dude Perfect, sit next to them and enjoy their stunts...then go out in the yard and have a bottle flipping contest. **These actions let your kids know you care about what they are interested in**—and ultimately these fun moments can help your kids keep their eyes on what matters most: the life right in front of them.

WESTARTNOW.ORG

ADDITIONAL**RESOURCES**

For Actor/Artist/Author Brady Smith, raising kids in Hollywood is about more than just the big screen; it's about **finding balance with your little screen, so you don't miss out on the biggest screen of all—life.** In Screen Sanity Episode 6, Brady shares thoughts about the relationship between screens, creativity, and making family memories your kids will always cherish.

Listen along at **westartnow.org/podcast**

Are you looking for a fun way to encourage your family to stay captivated by life not screens? When you wear your shirt, you help spread our message AND proceeds benefit the nonprofit mission of START—helping families raise happy, healthy kids in an increasingly digital world.

Grab your swag at **westartnow.org/merch**

Ready to find a healthier screen-life balance? Our **Family Fun Downloads** are light-hearted activities to help build stronger connections with your kids and community.

Join the fun at **westartnow.org/family-fun**

We were recently reminded by Lin-Manuel Miranda of another good old fashioned trick that can be considered time well spent—time alone. In an interview with *GQ magazine*, Miranda credited his unattended childhood afternoons with fostering inspiration.

"I have fond memories of pretending ninjas were going to come into every room of the house and thinking to myself, 'What is the best move to defend myself? How will I 'Home Alone' these ninjas?' I was learning to create incredible flights of fancy...

Unless you learn how to be in your head, you'll never learn how to create. Because there is nothing better to spur creativity than a blank page or an empty bedroom."

LIN-MANUEL MIRANDA / CREATOR OF HAMILTON

DIVE DEEPER

While the first six videos cover our top five rules of thumb for digital health, videos 7-10 dive deeper into pain points that might be striking a nerve in your family these days.

VIDEO 07
STARTING THE CONVO

Ready to make changes with screens but not sure where to start?
This video offers step-by-step ideas for getting the whole family on board.

PAGE 59

VIDEO 08
BROKEN CONNECTIONS

A closer look at how screens can accidentally damage relationships
and a hopeful conversation on repairing them.

PAGE 67

VIDEO 09
SOCIAL MEDIA PREP

A video for parents of kids who are dipping their toes into the social media
world. Let's get prepped and ready for the road ahead!

PAGE 75

VIDEO 10
VIDEO GAME MELTDOWNS

Noticing how video games tend to suck your child in? This video
offers a fresh approach to finding balance, reducing explosions and
avoiding game addiction.

PAGE 83

DIVE DEEPER

VIDEO 07 /
STARTING THE CONVO

A recent DoSomething.org survey
found that

only 14%
of youth have
had helpful
conversations

with adults about the digital world.

Use your smartphone's camera app to

SCAN HERE TO WATCH VIDEO 07

or go to westartnow.org/screen-sanity-portal

SESSION**RECAP**

We hope Screen Sanity has given you plenty of ideas to try, but before you go home and make bold, sweeping changes with your family, we'd suggest you kick off the topic with **two starter conversations:** the first where you cast vision as a family, and the second where you get curious about ways screens are affecting that vision. This helps prep the soil for the practical steps you want to take with screens—and these convos can make meaningful memories.

PAUSE**+REFLECT**

What stood out to you?

GROUP**DISCUSSION 01**

Pause a moment to jot down ideas in the Family Screen Plan on the next page—no pressure if you need to leave a few blanks. Then share with your group: **What's one practical step you plan to take to lead your family towards digital health? Or what is something new you've tried recently with screens and how's it going?**

GROUP**DISCUSSION 02**

Some parenting conversations can feel awkward and even scary—and can cause a bit of analysis-paralysis.

On a scale of 1-10, how confident do you feel talking with your kids about screentime? What hesitations or obstacles do you have about diving into this topic?

IN YOUR WORDS

"I will admit, the first few evenings, it was hard for me to enforce a new screentime limit because it meant I had another battle to fight when all I wanted to do was wind down as I cooked dinner.

But, because of our new rule, my daughter started finding her way to the kitchen, hanging out with me at the dinner table, lingering a little longer each night. The conversations had more substance (6-year-old substance). We discussed happenings on the playground and bus, what her teacher talked about and finally BOYS! We connected about the things she is noticing, learning, and feeling about the world. **I realized that it wasn't just me who was missing out; it was both of us.**"

Mendy M. | START Parent

FAMILY SCREEN PLAN

Cast a vision

Values or mantras to guide
our family through this
season:

_____

_____

_____

Accountability

Filters, monitoring services +
practices we'll use as safety
nets:

_____

_____

_____

Start with yourself

Friction points to help me
model healthy screen use:

_____

_____

_____

Ride. Practice. Drive.

Ways to increase responsibility
over time:

_____

_____

_____

Tables + Bedtimes

The spaces + times our
devices will recharge:

_____

_____

_____

Time well spent

Meaningful activities to help
us grow stronger:

_____

_____

_____

LEADING WITH HONESTY *by* Jeff B. | START Parent

My wife and I have three kids, middle school and older, and for years we haven't really felt prepared to talk to them about their digital lives. The truth is, their young brains—filled with neuroplasticity—understand the digital world in a way that is hard for us to keep up with. They are digital natives. And trying to keep up feels like learning a second language at an old age.

So, because we feel overwhelmed and already one step behind, we are often tempted to give up and let them figure this thing out on their own. But, this changed for us a couple of years ago, when good friends of ours sent their daughter to college and overnight, lost contact with her.

It took them two years of searching before they were able to contact her again. When they did, they learned that while she was in high school, under their roof, she had developed an online friendship with a person—and then a group of people—who were antisocial, to put it nicely. As their high school daughter developed a bond with this group, she began to plot a move to runaway and join them, and used "going away to college" as an opportunity to escape.

It was devastating. As parents, there is just no way you can predict the kind of paths that our kids might choose to walk down, and the internet has opened up paths for them that are even more unpredictable and honestly, scary.

But in the aftermath, my wife and I began to look at our kids' digital lives in the face and come to grips with a truth: We will never be experts in this part of parenting. We will never be one step ahead of this game. Generations before us have been mostly prepared to understand and be able to predict the types of pitfalls kids will fall in. That is no longer the case, but it doesn't mean that we can look the other way when we get overwhelmed.

Instead, we have started being super honest with our kids, telling them, **"Listen, we actually don't know what we are doing, but that's not gonna stop us from doing our best. We are with you, and we are for you, and we will figure this thing out as we go."**

Just saying this aloud to them has given us and them the freedom and motivation to have conversations that have been honest and rich, drawing us closer as a family. There have been times where we have made a rule for their phones out of fear, and a few months later, we've learned that those rules were unnecessary. And there have been times where we've made rules that we look back and breathe a huge sigh of relief that we stuck to our guns.

We don't have to be experts to enter into this process. That is actually not even an option. But we've learned that admitting our lack of expertise to our kids has actually built a bridge that we are hoping will last well into their adult lives.

The road our kids are walking is hard, and they need us to join them on it, even if we don't have all of the answers.

JEFF B. / START PARENT

DIVE DEEPER

VIDEO 08 /
BROKEN CONNECTIONS

We have all experienced the pain of "technoference", but it is never too late to rebuild relationships with each other.

We must learn to offer our loved ones our ~~full face.~~

Use your smartphone's camera app to
SCAN HERE TO WATCH **VIDEO 08**

or go to westartnow.org/screen-sanity-portal

SESSION**RECAP**

When we offer our kids our attention, we offer them the safety to explore the world, try new things and build trust. But when we are distracted, we accidentally send them the message that they are not a priority. This digital divide can lead to emotional damage—and while the thought of this is overwhelming, it is not beyond repair. **Restoring connection with loved ones is not always easy, but it is worthwhile.**

PAUSE**+REFLECT**

What stood out to you?

GROUP**DISCUSSION 01**

As much as we love to do huge, ground shaking things to show our children we love them, it's not the big, spectacular moments that matter most. The simple, tiny, everyday actions add up—tying our kids shoes, reading with them, writing a note of encouragement. And yet—these tiny things can be exhausting!

What's a small way you try to give your kids attention— and what is challenging about it?

GROUP**DISCUSSION 02**

Has your child ever called you out for allowing your screen to cause "technoference"? How did you respond? Is there anything you would change?

TAKE HOME TIP
NARRATE YOUR PHONE ACTIVITIES

As children in an analog world, we had visible windows into the tasks our parents were doing. When they scheduled playdates, they walked to the wall calendar. When they read the news, we heard the swish of the newspaper. Today's kids don't have the same visibility into our tasks, making it easy for them to assume when we pick up our phones that we are simply zoning out.

One way to give them cues is to narrate the tasks we are accomplishing on our phones. **This not only signals to our kids that we aren't ignoring them, but also helps them understand that screens can be beautiful tools for connection** when used with intention and purpose. Bonus: it helps hold us accountable to not get sucked in!

From the time we are born, our brains are hard-wired for connection.

Research in orphanages where infants are deprived of attention reveals that when babies aren't shown attention, they fail to thrive.* Throughout childhood, human connection remains the foundation upon which love, security, and confidence are built.

In 2017, the city of Boston asked all kindergarteners across the city to design the best playground imaginable. The planners envisioned twisty slides, splash pads and sand pits. But, to their surprise, the overwhelming top request from the kindergarteners? That the playgrounds would require lockers for their parents to put away their phones. **The main thing the kids wanted from the playground was quality time with their parents.**

That said, today's parents are in a double bind: the same device that causes interference is also the device that helps us care for our kids. There is no perfect solution.

So take a deep breath, and give yourself grace. It's okay to tell your kids to go out and play while you send emails or complete a task on your computer for work. In today's world, this is often necessary and can even be healthy as children grow older and more independent. But take care to not let these moments eclipse times of intentional presence and attunement to your child's emotional health..and when damage occurs, take time to make amends.

* Harvard University Press 2014

SHARENTING *by* Lauri C. | START Parent

I have five kids ages 16 down to 5, and my girls are getting to that age when they mostly look at me like I am crazy. It's a thing. They are actually growing up.

And as they've grown, I've learned to change and adapt a lot of things, including what I share on social media. It's like a negotiation: they allow me to take pictures of them on their first day of high school, but I promise I won't share it. It is a little hard sometimes to curb my desire to post about them on Facebook, but I keep my promise because they are getting close to adulthood, and I'm beginning to think about life after they flee the nest. So, even though I want to show the whole world how proud I am of these girls, I keep it to myself. I have to let go. And it's fine... it's time.

But what really caught me off guard was a pattern I started noticing in my nine year old. Sometimes, we would be out and about—at a Royals game or picking apples at a local orchard—and I would line up my crew like I always do for a selfie. But before he would jump in, he would stop me, look me in the eye, and say, "Mom, are you going to post this?"

At first, I shrugged off his pleas but the more it happened, the more I began thinking about him, and really trying to see the world through his eyes. He is a private guy to begin with—the type that doesn't like to be called on in class if he doesn't know the answer. Anytime I put the spotlight on him, he feels like he's in his underwear in public. It's just how he's wired.

One afternoon last fall, when I went to pick him up at school, he walked outside at the same time another mom was telling me how "hysterical that post was." (I had posted about his five year old brother stacking 22 rolls of toilet paper and I'll be honest, it was funny!) I posted it because I thought it was innocent. No one was exposed. And it felt good to make people laugh.

Until my nine year old caught my arm, looked me in the eye, and asked, "Mama, what did you post? What did you share?" So, the thing is, this mom and I were laughing at what my five year old had done, but my nine year old? What he heard was a couple of mamas poking fun at a member of our family. Without permission. I could feel his anxiety rising and his trust wavering.

I think so often when we talk about social media we tend to think the only thing affecting today's teens is how they interact with other teens. **But I'm learning that the pressures don't only come from their friends; it can also come from me as a parent.**

So have I gone dark on Facebook altogether? No. But I have started trying to make sure I always ask my kids for permission before I post.

Sharenting.

Verb.

A combination of two words: parenting and sharing. Specifically oversharing — on social media.

DIVE DEEPER

VIDEO 09 /
SOCIAL MEDIA PREP

In the past, when asked what they want to be when they grow up, kids would say an astronaut. A lawyer. A nurse.

86% of today's kids say they are interested in becoming a social media influencer.

Use your smartphone's camera app to
SCAN HERE TO WATCH VIDEO 09

or go to westartnow.org/screen-sanity-portal

SESSION**RECAP**

Whether your kids are dipping their toes into the social media world, or that milestone is still several years away, **now is a good time to start "driver's ed" for social media.** Before they snap, you should chat—and open the door for ongoing conversations about pornography, bullying, and social comparison. When it's time for a learner's permit—start with strong limits, give them lots of coaching and gradually give them more freedom to use the app independently. As you trust them to merge into traffic, make sure they know you are a safe place to come when accidents and injuries occur.

PAUSE**+REFLECT**

What stood out to you?

GROUP**DISCUSSION 01**

One of the most powerful ways to connect with our kids is to step into their shoes and see the world through their eyes.

As you think about your own experiences in social media, what do you think makes it so appealing to kids and adults alike? What are the benefits?

GROUP**DISCUSSION 02**

As you reflect on your own childhood, what experiences are you grateful happened before social media was invented? How do these memories help you relate to your child's world?

TAKE HOME TIP
THE UNSPOKEN RULEBOOK

Did you know there is an unspoken "rulebook" for our kids on social media? This book isn't published; it's written on our kids' hearts. Girls should be tall, but not too tall. Hair long and shiny, but not too shiny. Body curvy, but not with a six-pack. Don't mess up, or you may never get a job.

Ask your child to share with you what "rules" they consider to be unbreakable in the social media world. Once they are able to articulate these rules, they will be better able to see through them and **separate their own self-worth from social media's false standard of perfection.**

TikTok is the new king of social media—more popular than Facebook and Instagram—and used by kids an average of

87 minutes per day.

Qustodio's 2021 Annual Report

For private conversations, Snapchat is still very much a thing. This popular app is used by up to

90 percent of 13-24 year olds.

Vox.com

According to ex-Facebook employees, the company has internal data that Instagram is toxic for teen girls—making

body image worse

for 1 of 3 girls. Among teens who reported suicidal thoughts, 13% of British users traced the desire to kill themselves to Instagram.

Wall Street Journal

ADDITIONAL**RESOURCES**

Amanda Mozea is the former Education Outreach Manager at Media Girls, where she and her team worked to help girls to think critically about how to show up authentically in their social media feeds. In Episode 5 of the Screen Sanity podcast, Amanda joins us to share thoughts about the conversations parents need to have with their daughters to help them swim—not sink—in their social worlds.

Listen along at **westartnow.org/podcast**

Amy is a student at Cornell University and the co-author with her dad, Andy Crouch, of *My Tech Wise Life: Growing Up and Making Choices in a World of Devices.* If you're a parent who is struggling with worry that waiting for social media might cause them to "miss out" or be "left behind" their peers, Amy shares what it was like growing up with digital limits, and gratitude for the ways those limits protected her from social pressures, distraction, and harmful secrets. A great one to listen to with your tweens or teens!

Listen along at **westartnow.org/podcast**

When Cierra Karson overheard her preschool daughter saying her daily affirmations in the mirror, it made her cry happy tears, because she knew that one day, this little girl would have the confidence she needs to navigate the challenges she will face in the social media world. In this blog, Cierra shares why and how this young family makes this practice a part of their everyday routine.

Check it out at **westartnow.org/blog**

READY TO DIVE IN?
GRAB YOUR COPY OF THE SOCIAL MEDIA PLAYBOOK

If you are looking for a way to start a conversation with your tween or teen about the world of social media, we've got you covered. This little workbook is designed to help you mentor your child into the social media world.

The Social Media Playbook is a tool for setting intentions, drawing boundaries, and sparking conversations to help kids (and adults!) stay healthy on their social media journey. We don't recommend you assign this to your kid as an independent study, but see it as the perfect excuse to sit down and connect—sharing the good, the bad, and the ugly of what you've experienced in social media. It's short, but meaty, so don't rush through it in one setting—some families find one lesson per week is a good pace. Best paired with a bowl of ice cream!

Download your free copy at
westartnow.org/social-media-playbook
or grab a printed copy on Amazon ($10).
Also available in Spanish.

IN YOUR WORDS

"Even though I've worked with youth professionally for most of my career, I still find it challenging to mentor my own teens in the world of social media. I just don't know what questions to ask. This playbook is a godsend—I went through it with my teen and it resulted in some of the most rich, meaningful conversations we've ever had. I'm so grateful and will be sharing it with all of my friends."

JOEL M. | START PARENT

DIVE DEEPER

VIDEO 10 /
VIDEO GAME MELTDOWNS

In the 2020 pandemic, kids in the US played Roblox an average of

100 minutes per day.

With video games being an occasional lifesaver and a way to play with friends, it's more important than ever to mentor your child in the gaming world, helping to counterbalance their addictive properties.

QUSTODIO'S 2021 ANNUAL REPORT

Use your smartphone's camera app to

SCAN HERE TO WATCH VIDEO 10

or go to westartnow.org/screen-sanity-portal

SESSION**RECAP**

While the content of video games invites a variety of opinions — especially when it comes to first-person shooter games — our goal in this session is to help your child **avoid addiction and enjoy games with balance.** Video games cause kids' brain activity to speed up and become out of sync with the world. (Read: raging tantrums.) By the time your kids flee the nest, you want them to identify this pattern and self-regulate their video game habits. This means understanding their personal limits, and transitioning off the video game before their brains and bodies begin to meltdown.

PAUSE**+REFLECT**

What stood out to you?

GROUP**DISCUSSION 01**

Remember riding a merry-go-round as a child? Round and round you'd go, faster and faster and when you hopped off the world still spun even though you now stood on solid ground.

Neurotherapist Susan Dunaway shares that when our kids are asked to "hop off" screens they can feel like we did after that spin on the merry-go-round. **Describe a time when you witnessed this phenomenon—or experienced it yourself.**

GROUP**DISCUSSION 02**

What are some tricks you've found helpful for reducing video game meltdowns?

TAKE HOME TIP
TRANSITION WITH TOUCH

When it's time to get off, we recommend that you don't jerk the console cord out of the wall or slam their laptop closed. Instead, allow them to finish the level they have been working on. Maybe try language like, "find a good place to stop."

Another great trick is to help their brain reconnect with their body by touching them. Just placing your hand on their shoulder or sitting next to them on the couch to "wake them up"...or maybe you challenge them to a pushup contest.

And the best place to send them for a reset? Outside! **There are many benefits to time outdoors,** including the role sun exposure has in improving our mood – especially important these days.

UNDERSTANDING YOUR CHILD'S BRAIN

1 **Still developing**

The pre-frontal cortext is the last part of the brain to mature at about age 25. It is responsible for decision-making, higher reasoning, judgment and self-control. Until our kids' brains are fully wired, they need loving, supportive adults to help them navigate the fallout of video games—and develop healthy, self-regulated gaming habits.

2 **Pumped + primed**

Teens' brains are pumped and primed to seek and take in new experiences. Think of them like a brand new Lamborghini that is loaded with gas and revved up—and unsure where to go. This developmental stage helps them leave home as young adults, but also makes them vulnerable to risky and addictive behaviors, like compulsive gaming.

3 **Flexible**

Our children's brains are full of plasticity. They are capable of changing, growing and learning new skills—and able to respond to treatment. If your child is exhibiting signs of gaming addiction—a decrease in grades, sleep, concentration or social interaction—help is available. Seek out a cognitive behavioral therapy (CBT) program in your area.

SUPPORTING YOUR CHILD'S BRAIN

Whether your child sets his own timer or you set it for him (or her), make sure the "finish line" is a number of minutes that doesn't overload his brain. Our Video Game Decision Tree can help families get on the same page about time limits.

Download it now at **westartnow.org/resources**

The #1 indicator that your child's brain has reached its gaming limit is behavior change.

If your child is able to transition off his game calmly and go about his day, you've likely found an appropriate time limit for him or her.

But, anytime he responds with a behavior change—irritability, decreased concentration, arguments and meltdowns—that's a good sign that his brain is overloaded, and next time you need to reduce the time limit.

Our Video Game Decision Tree helps families get on the same page about time limits. You can download a printable copy to share with your kids, and maybe even hang near the gaming station as a reminder of what you are striving for!

CAN I GAME?

Yes! Set your timer
Ex: 30 minutes for 10 year old / 60 minutes for 15 year old*

No.
Suggest a different activity

Self-Regulated
Child sets timer & turns off own game.

Parent-Regulated
"Hey kiddo, it's time to get off."

Irritable Behavior
"But I just gotta do this!" or reduced ability to concentrate

Next time: Yes!
30 minutes / 60 minutes

Calm Behavior
"Okay Mom! Can I finish up this level?"

Fold down computer
"I love your brain too much to argue. Time to play outside!"

Next time: Yes!
30 minutes / 60 minutes

Next time: Yes!
Reduce time in half

Sneaking games?
Lose privileges for 24-48 hours. Reintroduce in 10 minute increments.

* Older teens can have more time but their brains still need a break at least once per hour. Go on a walk, do push-ups or grab a healthy snack to reset. *Created in consultation with Susan Dunaway, Amend Neurocounseling.*

Onward!

We hope this journey has helped you gather fresh ideas for digital health. You might have new goals and changes you want to make—and while these things are worth celebrating, make sure you give yourself grace if your new plans don't play out the way you imagined.

When you run into challenges, the best thing you can do is take a step back, revisit this book, reach out to others in your group for support, and try again!

If this content has been helpful for you, consider hosting your own Screen Sanity group! We've included tips on pages 92-95 to help you get started.

You were never meant to do life alone—so let's continue this journey together. If you haven't already, download our additional resources at **westartnow.org/resources** and we'll stay in touch with tips and tricks to help you navigate the digital world.

We are a 501(c)3 nonprofit, and we depend on people like you to expand our reach, deepen our impact and equip parents across the globe with the tools they are hungry for. If you want to be part of this mission, you can give at **westartnow.org/donate.**

 @we.start.now    @westartnow.org

SCREEN SANITY 101
OUR BASIC STRUCTURE

3
GATHERINGS

2
HOURS

2
VIDEOS EACH

We recommend discussing videos 1-6 to build a foundation of digital health. Then, if you want to dive deeper into a certain topic, you can add videos 7-10.

OTHER WAYS TO DO IT

The Kickstart Event
1 Gathering • 90 Minutes • 2 Videos

Pro-tip: Watch and discuss two videos at the event, then encourage parents to complete the rest at home, after the kids are tucked into bed.

The Weekly Meet-Up
6 Gatherings • 30 Minutes • 1 Video

Pro-tip: To maximize discussion time, have group members watch the video before your gathering.

IDEAS FOR GATHERING

Wine and cheese night

Meet at a coffee shop/playground

Parent night with your PTO

Lunch + Learn with co-workers

HOW TO SHOW UP*

Be Curious

We are the first generation of parents raising kids who would rather text than talk. There is no handbook for parenting in the digital world—so rather than feeling pressure to "know it all" or "be right," stay curious about how to "get it right."

Be Authentic

We encourage you to be vulnerable and honest about struggles. When we show up authentically, we invite creativity, belonging and connection with others.

Be Empathetic

Be quick to step into your group members' shoes, and see the world through their eyes. You'll find that most parents are lonely and weary of fighting battles against their kids. Take this opportunity to stand together and fight for our kids.

*Inspired by Brene Brown, *Daring Greatly*

EXAMPLE SCHEDULE

Here's how one host structured her two-hour window:

7:00	Gathering together
7:15	Welcome + Introductions
7:30	Video One (12 min)
7:45	Group Discussion (25 min)
8:10	Video Two (15 min)
8:25	Group Discussion (25 min)
8:50	Farewells

"Hey friend! I'm hosting a casual gathering with a few friends (six-ish) this Wednesday to check out a new study about kids and screentime. I know this is a struggle in our home and I want to get together and talk about it! Are you available that evening?"

A sample invitation. Feel free to copy, paste and tweak!

PLAN YOUR GATHERING

Invite with purpose*

In your invitations or promotions, be clear about the purpose of the gathering. This helps people know what to expect and allows them to "opt out" if they aren't interested. If you have specific requests about food, drink, social distancing—share them up front!

Who to invite

Other parents, coaches, and leaders whose paths intersect your own in a meaningful and regular way. Group members do NOT need to all be in the same parenting stage—it's powerful to learn from others who are in a different place than you!
Circles to consider:

🎾	Sports teams	⛪	Church
🧭	Girl/Boy scouts	🏫	School
🩰	Dance class	👪	PTA
⛺	Summer camp	📚	Book club

*Inspired by *The Art of Gathering* by Priya Parker

1 Start with why

To open your gathering, take a moment to share "why" you are here. Whether it is a personal painpoint you are experiencing with your kids, or a life-long interest in the role of technology, sharing your story builds trust, authenticity and safety for your group.

2 Pause + reflect

At the end of each video, there is a slide inviting participants to pause, reflect, and jot down a note or two before starting the discussion. Don't rush through this! This critical step allows participants to take note of personal learnings before they hear thoughts of group members.

3 You go first

When it's time for videos and discussion questions, don't be afraid to go first. When you share openly about the challenges you are facing at home, you help other people feel comfortable sharing. After you share, try going around the circle, giving people the option to "pass." This helps ensure that everyone has a chance for their voice to be heard.

4

Resist the urge to fix-it

If the conversation gets intense or uncomfortable, release yourself from the pressure to solve every problem. (Unless you are a liscensed therapist—then by all means, go for it!) Try transitioning out of intense conversations with language like, "Thanks for sharing. I don't know the answers, but maybe we can take a look at some of the other resources westartnow.org has provided to see what they have to offer.

5

Follow up

After the gathering, check in with your group to see how it's going. Even a simple text message can be powerful—and can be a model for your kids of how to maximize the gift of technology. We aren't meant to do life alone, and these small acts of kindness can help heal a world plagued by loneliness and disconnection.

6

Stay connected

You are facilitating this study because you have a heart for people and a willingness to address a great need.
The questions that will surface are tough, and you might not know all the answers. You might even end up with more questions! We're here to help. Register at **westartnow.org/ screen-sanity-group-study** to join our community of leaders, where you will receive ongoing support and exclusive opportunities to interact with our team. You are not alone!

westartnow.org

Made in United States
North Haven, CT
13 April 2022